HEALING
A CHILD'S
GRIEVING HEART

Also by Alan Wolfelt:

Creating Meaningful Funeral Ceremonies:
A Guide for Families

Healing a Friend's Grieving Heart:
100 Practical Ideas for Helping Someone
You Love Through Loss

Understanding Your Grief:
Ten Essential Touchstones for Finding
Hope and Healing Your Heart

The Wilderness of Grief: Finding Your Way

Healing Your Grieving Heart for Kids:
100 Practical Ideas

The Journey Through Grief:
Reflections on Healing

Companion Press is dedicated to the education and support of both the bereaved and bereavement caregivers.

We believe that those who companion the bereaved by walking with them as they journey in grief have a wondrous opportunity: to help others embrace and grow through grief—and to lead fuller, more deeply-lived lives themselves because of this important ministry.

Companion
PRESS

For a complete catalog and ordering information, write or call:

Companion Press
The Center for Loss and Life Transition
3735 Broken Bow Road
Fort Collins, CO 80526
(970) 226-6050
www.centerforloss.com

HEALING
A CHILD'S
GRIEVING HEART

·

100 IDEAS FOR FAMILIES,
FRIENDS & CAREGIVERS

·

ALAN D. WOLFELT, PH.D.

Companion
PRESS

Fort Collins, Colorado
An imprint of the Center for Loss and Life Transition

Companion Press is an imprint of the
Center for Loss and Life Transition,
3735 Broken Bow Road, Fort Collins, Colorado 80526
970-226-6050
www.centerforloss.com

Companion Press books may be purchased in bulk for
sales promotions, premiums or fundraisers. Please
contact the publisher at the above address for more
information.

Printed in the United States of America

21 20 19 18 17   10 9 8 7 6

ISBN: 978-1-879651-28-9

For my high school music teacher, Mr. Jeager, who unknowingly supported me and thousands of youth in ways he may never have imagined. If only all children could come to know a Mr. Jeager.

INTRODUCTION

If you are reading this book, you are making a commitment to help a grieving child. Perhaps you are a parent who is not only mourning the death of your spouse, but concerned about helping your children mourn well. Perhaps you are a teacher with a student who has experienced the death of a grandparent, parent, sibling, or friend. Perhaps you work in a hospice or funeral home where you have the opportunity to help children in grief. Whatever your relationship to grieving kids, you are probably asking yourself, "What can I do to help?"

This book's 100 practical ideas are a response to that very question. Some of the ideas will teach you the basic principles of grief and mourning. The remainder offer practical, here-and-now tips for spending time with and actively supporting the grieving child. They will help you put your compassion into action. They will help you know what to do when you don't know what to do.

You'll also notice that each of the 100 ideas suggests a *carpe diem*, which means, as fans of the movie *Dead Poets Society* will remember, "seize the day." My hope is that you will not relegate this book to your shelves but keep it handy on your nightstand or desk. Pick it up often and turn to any page; the carpe diem suggestion will help you seize the day by helping the grieving child today, right now, right this minute. If you come to an idea that doesn't seem to fit you or the child, simply ignore it and flip to a different page.

A Word About Play

As you read through the 100 ideas, you'll find that I encourage
you to play with the grieving child, to spend time with her
doing the things that she likes to do. You see, I believe that play
is the grieving child's natural method of self-expression and
communication.

Children often use play in response to losses because they are
trying to learn about what no one can teach them. It is through
their play that they have taught me about the meaning of death
in their lives. For grieving kids, "playing out" their grief thoughts
and feelings is a natural and self-healing process. Remember:
Kids often mourn more through their behaviors—including their
play—than they do through words.

To deny play to a grieving child is to deny him the ability to mourn
and heal. Children are sometimes denied play when the adults
around them consider play a waste of time. In fact, many adults
perceive play as self-indulgent and think children who play too
much are being spoiled. How can a hurting child feel it's OK to
play when he hears messages like, "You need to take care of your
Mom now" or "Be the man of the house now." These kinds of
messages emphasize that this is no time for play, but instead a time
for a child to be serious.

Play allows the grieving child to be accepted for where she is in her
emotional state at any given moment in time. Play is where she
lives while she mourns. In instinctively moving toward play, she
creates a personal experience where she can "let go" and respond
to herself, to others, and to her world. If she is discouraged from
play, she moves into regimentation and loses her confidence and
ability for self-expression.

A very wise person once said, "Play is the child's response to life."
In my experience, I think we could also add that play is often the
child's normal, natural and healing response to death.

A Caution

Sometimes, despite the ideas and support offered by this book, you won't know how to help the grieving child. Maybe the child isn't responding to your help. Or perhaps he doesn't seem to be moving forward in his grief journey. Maybe you try some of the 100 ideas and the suggested activities stimulate thoughts and feelings in the child that you don't know how to handle.

When you start to feel in over your head, don't hesitate to seek professional assistance for the child. Such a step is not an admission of failure, it's an expression of love for the child. A good counselor will not only help the child, she'll help you understand what's going on and how you can continue to help.

Each one of us is inextricably involved in the mystery we call life, and the exciting reality is that we can influence its path. Each one of us is capable of having a positive impact on the emotional and spiritual lives of grieving kids. Each one of us has the privilege of sharing love and of helping children meet the six needs of mourning outlined in this book. Helping a child mourn not only helps the child, it helps the world as a whole. Thank you for joining me in my efforts to make a difference in the lives of grieving children.

Alan D. Wolfelt, Ph.D.

1.

UNDERSTAND THE DIFFERENCE BETWEEN GRIEF AND MOURNING

- Grief is the constellation of internal thoughts and feelings we experience when someone loved dies.

- Mourning is the outward expression of our grief. Mourning is necessary for healing to take place.

- I often refer to children as "forgotten mourners." Why? Because though all children grieve when someone loved dies, we (as a society, as families and often as individuals) rarely encourage them to mourn.

- You can help the grieving child you love by encouraging her to mourn. You can be the person she feels "safe" to mourn in the presence of.

CARPE DIEM

Think about your own experiences with grief. Did you mourn? If so, what ways of mourning were helpful to you?

2.

OBSERVE THAT KIDS MOURN MORE THROUGH BEHAVIORS THAN WORDS

- Often grieving children don't talk and talk about their feelings. Instead, they act them out.

- For example, the child may act mopey and lethargic but may not have the words to pinpoint how he's feeling or why, specifically, he's feeling that way.

- Watch for mourning behaviors in kids. A child who is feeling confused might get easily upset. A child who is angry about the death might misbehave or pick fights with other kids.

- Children also mourn through their play. Watch for their feelings to come out in the ways they pretend, relate to other kids, physically move, create artwork, etc.

CARPE DIEM

Spend some time simply observing the grieving child today. What can you learn by watching him just "be"?

3.

UNDERSTAND THE SIX NEEDS OF MOURNING

Need 1. Acknowledge the reality of the death.

- The child must gently confront the reality that someone she loved is dead and will never physically be present to her again.

- Children tend to accept the reality of a death in "doses." That is, they let in just a little of the pain at a time then return to their play or other distractions. This "dosing" of grief is not only normal but necessary, for it makes the early days of grief bearable.

- Help the child understand what "dead" physically means. Explain that the body can no longer think, feel, hear, breathe, etc. and will never be "alive" again.

- Whether the death was sudden or anticipated, the child may take years to fully integrate the reality of the loss. As she gets older and matures developmentally, the death will take on new layers of meaning and greater depth.

CARPE DIEM

Today, talk about the physical reality of the death. Make sure the child understands how and why the person died.

4.

UNDERSTAND THE SIX NEEDS OF MOURNING

Need 2. Feel the pain of the loss.

• Like all mourners, children need to embrace the pain of the loss. Fortunately, most children haven't yet learned how to repress or deny their feelings. If they're sad, they generally allow themselves to be sad.

• You can help by encouraging the child to talk about his painful thoughts and feelings and by being a nonjudgmental listener.

• You can also model your own grief feelings. If you're sad, express your sadness in the child's presence.

• Children will naturally "dose" their pain. Support this child as he allows his pain in, little by little.

CARPE DIEM

The next time the child cries, resist the natural urge to encourage him to stop crying. Instead, hold him gently and let him cry as long and hard (and as often) as he wants to.

5.

UNDERSTAND THE SIX NEEDS OF MOURNING

Need 3. Remember the person who died.

- When someone loved dies, they live on in us through memory.

- Grieving children need to actively remember the person who died and help commemorate the life that was lived.

- Never try to take away a child's memories in a misguided attempt to save her from pain. It's good for the child to continue to look at photos or videotapes of the person who died. It's good for her to share stories of the person's life and to hear other people talk about the person who died, too.

- Remembering the past makes hoping for the future possible.

CARPE DIEM

Invite the child to tell you about a memory of the person who died. Or ask the child to show you a snapshot of the person who died then tell you what was going on when the picture was taken.

6.

UNDERSTAND THE SIX NEEDS OF MOURNING

Need 4. Develop a new self-identity.

- Part of the child's self-identity was formed by the relationship he had with the person who died.

- Maybe he had a father and now he doesn't. Or maybe he was a big brother and now his younger sibling has died. How has the child's sense of who he is changed as a result of this death?

- No one can "fill in" for the person who died. Don't try to find a substitute father/best friend/grandparent/etc. for the child, at least not in the early months after the death. Supportive relationships—yes. Replacements—no!

- Sometimes grieving children are encouraged to take on roles and tasks that belonged to the person who died, yet forcing children to take on adult responsibilities will only hinder their healing process and unfairly steal their childhood from them.

CARPE DIEM

Ask the child to draw two pictures: one of his life before the death and one of his life after the death. Then talk with him about the differences depicted in the pictures.

7.

UNDERSTAND THE SIX
NEEDS OF MOURNING

Need 5. Search for meaning.

• When someone loved dies, we naturally question the meaning and purpose of life.

• Children tend to do this very simply through questions such as, "Why do people die?" and "What happens to people after they die?" and "Can Grandma go bowling in heaven?"

• Grieving kids will only feel free to ask these questions of adults whom they trust. Also be on the watch for the child's search for meaning in her play.

• Don't try to have answers to all the child's questions about the meaning of life. It's OK—even desirable—to admit that you struggle with the same issues.

CARPE DIEM

Share your beliefs about life and death and spirituality with the child without pressuring the child to believe what you believe.

8.

UNDERSTAND THE SIX NEEDS OF MOURNING

Need 6. Receive ongoing support from caring adults.

- Grief is a process—not an event. Children, like adults, will grieve long after the person has died.

- The grieving child needs your compassionate support and presence not only in the days and weeks following the death, but in the months and years to come.

- As they grow and mature developmentally, children will naturally grieve the death on new and ever deeper levels. If you can help the grieving child mourn as the need arises (even years after the death), you will be helping her grow into a healthy, loving adult.

CARPE DIEM

Create a plan to help this child throughout the next year. If you need to, mark regular dates to contact and spend time with her in your daily planner. Don't forget to make note of important dates, such as the child's birthday and the anniversary of the death.

9.

INCLUDE THE CHILD IN PLANNING AND CARRYING OUT THE FUNERAL

- Attending the funeral of someone loved is more than a privilege, it is a right. And anyone who loved the person who died should be encouraged to attend—even children.

- Children often don't know what to expect from a funeral. You can help by explaining what will happen before, during and after the ceremony. Let the child's questions and natural curiosity guide the discussion.

- Grieving kids often feel like their feelings "matter" when they can share a favorite memory or read a special poem as part of the funeral. Shyer children can participate by lighting a candle or placing something special (a memento, photo or drawing, for example) in or on the casket.

CARPE DIEM

If the funeral has already taken place, talk to the child about his experience with the ceremony. Help answer lingering questions and discuss ongoing ways for him to honor the person who died.

10.

HELP THE CHILD
CHOOSE A KEEPSAKE

- Following a death, survivors are often faced with the task of sorting through and disposing of the belongings of the person who died. Children should be included in this process when possible.

- Ask the grieving child if she would like to keep anything that belonged to the person who died. If the person who died was especially significant in her young life, you may want to box up other items and save them for appropriate times later in the child's life.

- Sometimes keepsakes can be stored in a "memory box" (see Idea 61) created especially for the child.

CARPE DIEM

Today, talk to the child about keepsakes. If she has already
selected one, ask her about its significance. If she hasn't,
help her make a plan for choosing and procuring one.

11.

GIVE THE CHILD PERMISSION TO FIND COMFORT IN "LINKING OBJECTS"

- "Linking objects" are simply items that belonged to the person who died in which the child takes comfort. They offer him a physical "link" to the person who died.

- Embrace the child's need to carry around or hold such linking objects. They help him feel closer to the person who died and provide some sense of safety and security.

- You may want to give the child a special linking object—maybe something he can wear like an article of clothing or a piece of costume jewelry.

CARPE DIEM

Does this child rely on a linking object right now? If so, talk to him about its significance. Affirm his need to have and hold this object.

12.

CONSIDER THE CHILD'S RELATIONSHIP TO THE PERSON WHO DIED

- Each child's response to a death depends largely upon the relationship she had with the person who died.

- For example, children will naturally grieve differently the deaths of a parent, a classmate and a grandparent.

- The closer the child felt to the person who died, the more difficult her grief is likely to be. Ambivalent or conflicted relationships can also complicate grief.

CARPE DIEM

Think about the child's relationship with the person who died—from her point of view. Set aside your own thoughts and feelings and enter her world as you consider this point.

13.

IF A CHILD'S PARENT HAS DIED, CONSIDER THIS

• The parent-child bond may be the strongest and most significant in life. When this bond is severed by death, the grieving child needs ample love and support.

• Perhaps the most important influence on the child's grief journey will be the response of the surviving parent, or other important adults in the child's life. While they cannot ignore their own grief and mourning, they must focus as much as possible on helping the child mourn.

• For the child, this death often results in many losses in addition to the loss of the parent, such as loss of financial stability or loss of a home and neighborhood friends if the family has to move.

CARPE DIEM

If the child's parent has died, help him capture his memories. Ask him to tell you about the parent, then, with his permission, help him write down his thoughts and feelings. He will treasure this record later in life.

14.

IF A CHILD'S SIBLING HAS DIED, CONSIDER THIS

- The death of a sibling is often among the most traumatic events in a child's life. Siblings' normal feelings for one another include not only love, but anger, jealousy and other ambivalent emotions.

- When a sibling dies, the surviving kids sometimes feel:

  - guilt (because they may have wished the sibling were gone at one time or another).

  - relief (because now they don't have to share or vie for attention).

  - fear (because now they know they could die, too).

  - confusion (because they're unsure if they're still a brother or sister).

- All of these feelings are normal. You can help by listening or observing nonjudgmentally as the child expresses them.

CARPE DIEM

If the child's sibling has died, help him write a poem in the sibling's honor. Have him write the sibling's name vertically on a piece of a paper, then begin each line of his poem with the corresponding letter.
For example,
My brother was my best friend
In all the world. He liked to fly
Kites and ride bike and play ball.
Early he died. I miss him so much.

15.

IF A CHILD'S GRANDPARENT HAS DIED, CONSIDER THIS

- When a grandparent dies, the grandchildren may or may not actively mourn; the intensity of their feelings depends on the closeness of the relationship they had with the grandparent who died.

- Sometimes when older people die, we deny or minimize our grief (and that of our children) because "it was time" or "he lived a long, full life." Even when these statements are true, we need to mourn and so do our children.

- The death of a grandparent or great-grandparent is often the first death a child experiences. Now is a good time to teach the child about funerals, spiritual beliefs regarding death and healthy mourning habits.

CARPE DIEM

If the grandparent died of age-related causes, make sure the child understands what happens to the human body as it gets old. Children understand and accept the natural cycle of life and death if it's presented to them in terms they understand.

16.

IF A CHILD'S FRIEND HAS DIED, CONSIDER THIS

- Children aren't supposed to die; we all feel that the natural order of life has been violated when a young person dies.

- When a peer dies, children not only lose the presence of someone they enjoyed spending time with, they also lose their sense of immortality. Now they know that they, too, could die at a young age.

- As with all types of deaths, be honest with the grieving child about how and why the friend has died. Don't hide or sugar-coat facts in an attempt to save the child from pain. Often, a child's imagination can conjure up explanations much scarier than reality.

CARPE DIEM

Help the child make a poster or collage about the child who died. He can assemble photos, drawings, words and even glue mementos to the paper backing. The child may want to hang the poster in his bedroom or present it to the parents of the child who died.

17.

CONSIDER THE NATURE OF THE DEATH

- The circumstances surrounding a death have a tremendous impact on a child's grief.

- Was the death sudden or anticipated? If sudden, was the death violent? How old was the person who died? Was this death stigmatized in some way (e.g. deaths from AIDS or suicide)?

- The more sudden the death, the more likely the child is to mourn in "doses" and push away some of the pain at first. Don't be surprised if the child responds with an apparent lack of feelings; he is merely protecting himself from the painful reality in the only way he knows how.

- Deaths of young people, violent deaths and stigmatized deaths tend to complicate grief for all survivors, young and old. Be especially supportive in these cases.

CARPE DIEM

Be honest with the child about the nature of the death.
Explain to her how the person died and why—as
best you can. Answer her questions honestly.

18.

LET THIS UNIQUE CHILD MOURN IN HER OWN WAY

- Each child has a unique personality that affects the ways in which she mourns. Some kids are talkative while others are quiet. Some are boisterous while others are placid. These personality styles, which existed long before the death, will influence the child's mourning.

- There is no "right" way to mourn. All mourning styles are OK, provided that the child hasn't changed dramatically due to the death.

- If, for instance, a formerly gregarious child withdraws completely from friends and family, this is a sign she needs extra grief help. The opposite is also true. If a formerly withdrawn child starts getting in fights, take it as a sign that she needs more help in getting her mourning needs met.

CARPE DIEM

Participate in the child's favorite activity with him, whether it be sports, art, whatever. "Walk with" the child as he mourns in his own way.

19.

CONSIDER THE AGE OF THE CHILD

- Younger children may not fully grasp the reality and finality of death, though many can and do if adults gently teach them.

- Older children may understand the physical reality of death but are only beginning to grasp the spiritual and emotional significance.

- As you talk about the death with the child, use words that he will understand. Don't talk down to him but do try to be clear and concrete. And always be as honest as you can.

CARPE DIEM

Think back to when you were the same age as the grieving child is now. What was your life like? What did you love? Hate? What made you feel safe? Afraid? This thought process might help you help the child.

20.

IF THE CHILD IS A GIRL, CONSIDER THIS

- Sometimes grieving girls are expected to cry and be sad all the time—but they're not allowed or taught to express their anger. Help the grieving child express all her grief thoughts and feelings without implying that some are OK and some are not.

- Sometimes grieving girls are expected to take over chores at home, especially if a parent dies. But children need to be children—especially grieving kids who already have a lot on their emotional plate.

CARPE DIEM

If others are pressuring this child to behave in a certain way because of her gender, supportively confront them about the inappropriateness of their demands.

21.

IF THE CHILD IS A BOY, CONSIDER THIS

- Sometimes grieving boys are told they have to "be strong" or "be a man" or, if one of the child's parents has died, "be the man of the house now."

- Boys are *not* men and shouldn't be expected to take on adult roles. If someone is pressuring a grieving boy to "be a man," maybe you can intervene and take some of the heat off.

- "Being strong" in grief just means postponing normal thoughts and feelings and complicating the child's life and compromising his happiness for years to come.

CARPE DIEM

If others are pressuring this child to behave in a certain way because of his gender, supportively confront them about the inappropriateness of their demands.

22.

IDENTIFY SAME-GENDER ADULT HELPERS FOR THE CHILD

- One important way to help grieving kids mourn is to provide them with good adult role models.

- By this age, kids are already identifying strongly with adults of their own gender.

- If a man is mourning this death openly, encourage him to spend time with the grieving boy. Help pair up a woman mourner with the grieving girl. Of course, this doesn't mean that adults of the opposite sex can't help grieving kids, too. They can and should!

CARPE DIEM

Today, identify a same-gender adult helper for this
child and talk to him or her about how to help.

23.

THINK ABOUT THE CHILD'S CULTURAL OR ETHNIC BACKGROUND

- The grieving child's response to death is influenced by her cultural and ethnic backgrounds. Different cultures are known for the various ways they express (or repress) their grief.

- Cultures that encourage outward expressions of grief are more likely to instill healthy mourning practices in grieving kids.

- Mourning-avoiding cultures, on the other hand, like those prevalent in American Anglo society today, often make a child's grief journey more difficult.

- Whatever the child's cultural or ethnic context, be respectful of its customs and beliefs.

CARPE DIEM

Think about your own cultural or ethnic background.
How it has influenced your grief and mourning?

24.

FEED THE CHILD'S BODY

- Grief stresses the heart, the mind and the body.

- In order to cope and feel as well as she can, the grieving child needs good foods right now.

- Make an effort to ensure that the child's diet isn't sabotaged by her own grief or her family's if they are (understandably) too preoccupied to worry about nutrition right now. Maybe you can coordinate volunteers to cook healthy meals for the family or do some grocery shopping for them.

CARPE DIEM

Treat the child to a home-cooked meal today.

25.

FEED THE CHILD'S SPIRIT

- Perhaps more important than feeding the grieving child's body is feeding his spirit. After all, grief is largely a spiritual journey.

- Teach the child about your spiritual beliefs and if appropriate, help him learn about the beliefs of other faiths as well.

- Invite the child to teach you about his spiritual beliefs.

- Some non-religious ways of feeding the grieving child's spirit include taking a walk in the woods, silently observing the night sky, or rowing a boat across a placid lake.

CARPE DIEM

Think about your own spiritual journey when you were a child. What helped you make sense of your spirituality?

26.

TEACH THE CHILD TO PRAY

- Prayer is a natural, healing response to loss.

- Prayer gives us an outlet for our innermost thoughts and feelings and gives us hope that maybe someone "out there"—God or whatever you might call him—is listening and will help us.

- Has the grieving child you care about been taught to pray? If not, maybe you can teach her how. (Be respectful of the child's family's religious beliefs. You may want to ask permission of the child's parents or guardian first.)

CARPE DIEM

Frame a short prayer for the child to hang near her bed.

27.

TALK WITH THE CHILD
ABOUT HEAVEN

- Depending on the child's spiritual upbringing, he may or may not believe in "heaven" per se, but he probably has some thoughts and feelings about what happens after death.

- Be his sounding board about this important issue. If he has doubts or fears, help him express them.

- If the child's faith teaches him that afterlife is a certainty, ask him what he thinks the afterlife is like. Often children will embellish their thoughts of heaven if asked, which can provide them some comfort.

- Some religions emphasize that death should be an event of celebration because the person goes on to eternal life. Even if the child believes this to be true, he still needs to mourn and embrace his painful feelings.

CARPE DIEM

Ask the child to draw a picture or write a short essay about what heaven is like. After, ask him to show/read it to you.

28.

THINK ABOUT OTHER LOSSES
THIS CHILD IS FACING

- Death and loss seldom occur in isolation. To understand the impact of a death on a child, you must also understand other losses the child may be experiencing at the same time.

- Has someone else the child loved died in the past? The child's grief for prior deaths may reappear now, compounding this loss.

- Stay sensitive to secondary losses, as well. These include loss of friends and community due to a geographical move, loss of security if the death has been financially draining on the family, loss of childhood if the child has been forced to "grow up" prematurely, etc.

CARPE DIEM

Make a list of other losses this child may be experiencing. Thinking about and creating this list will help you empathetically enter the child's world.

29.

GIVE THE GIFT OF PRESENCE

- The most important gift you can give the grieving child is your presence.

- You can't always *do* something special with or for the child, you can't always say something comforting, but you can be there for her.

- Especially if you are the child's parent or primary caregiver, try to spend as much time as possible with her in the early weeks and months following the death. Cut back on your working hours if you can; cancel evening meetings and weekend activities that don't involve the child. Your child needs you right now.

CARPE DIEM

Consider the difference between spending time with the child and simply being near the child (such as working at home while the child watches TV in another room). For the child's sense of security, both are important. However, the child especially needs you to focus on her right now.

30.

SURROUND THE CHILD WITH LOVE AND ACCEPTANCE

- Talk to all the important adults in the child's life about the importance of loving and supporting him right now.

- Call a meeting if you need to.

- Don't forget to talk to aunts and uncles, teachers, neighbors, coaches—anyone who has regular contact with the child.

CARPE DIEM

Make a list of all the key authority figures and role models in the child's life. Some of them may not even be aware of the death. Phone them today and connect the circle of love.

31.

HUG THE CHILD

- Physical touch is one of humanity's most healing gifts.

- If your relationship with the grieving child is close, hug him whenever you see him. At this age most children still like to be hugged. If this child is uncomfortable with touch, however, don't force it. Some children have had bad experiences with inappropriate touching.

- Use other appropriate forms of touch to show you care. Stroke the child's hair, rub his back, hold his hand.

CARPE DIEM

Make a point of touching the child today. Girls often like to have their hair combed or braided. Boys often like to wrestle.

32.

ENCOURAGE THE CHILD TO CRY

- Younger children naturally cry when they feel physical or emotional pain, but by the time they've entered school, many kids have learned that crying is a sign of weakness.

- Encourage this child to cry in your presence when she feels like it. Assure her that tears are a normal, necessary and healing form of mourning.

- You may feel like crying, too. Go ahead. Cry all you want and don't hide your tears from the child.

- However, if you are crying all the time and are concerned that your tears may be overwhelming the child, find a supportive adult to help you with your grief. By getting help for yourself, you'll also be helping the child.

CARPE DIEM

Observe how this child acts when she's on the verge of tears.
Does she cry openly or does she try to fight them back?

33.

BE A MODEL MOURNER

- Are you grieving this death, too? If so, you can be a model mourner for the child.

- Share appropriate thoughts and feelings with the grieving child. Don't burden him with too much adult pain, but be honest.

- In the presence of the child: cry; talk about the person who died; look at photo albums; be happy when you feel happy.

CARPE DIEM

How do you feel about the death today?
Express your feelings to the child.

34.

VISIT THE CEMETERY
WITH THE CHILD

- If the final resting place of the person who died is somewhere nearby, make it a point to visit the spot with the grieving child.

- The child may want to bring flowers or something she's made, like a card or a collage. Children can make gravestone rubbings or plant flower bulbs.

- As always, follow the child's lead during the visit. Talk if she wants to linger and talk. Explore with her if she wants to look around. Honestly answer her questions about what's happening to the body if the visit brings up questions or concerns.

CARPE DIEM

If she wants to, visit the cemetery with the child today.

35.

ENCOURAGE THE CHILD TO TALK ABOUT THE PERSON WHO DIED

• Talking about the person who died is an important form of mourning.

• Ask the child questions about the person who died. What is your first memory of him or her? What was your favorite thing about him or her? When was the last time you talked to him or her? What did he or she say?

• Don't bombard the child with too many questions or too much talk all at once. Save some for next time.

CARPE DIEM

Ask the child to tell you about a special memory he
has of the person who died. The more specific he can
be, the more he'll be keeping the memory alive.

36.

TAKE THE CHILD TO YOUR "MOURNING PLACE"

- Often grieving children respond well to ritual. Maybe you can find a certain place and time each week or month where the child feels safe to mourn.

- I sometimes shoot baskets with grieving kids or take them on walks in the mountains near my home. Whenever we begin our ritual activity, they know it's time to think about the loss and update me on how things are going.

- Some places to consider: a nearby park; a favorite restaurant; somewhere that was special to the person who died.

CARPE DIEM

Pick out a "mourning place" and take the child there today.

37.

USE THE NAME OF THE PERSON WHO DIED

- As you talk with the grieving child, use the name of the person who died comfortably and often.

- Hearing the name helps the child both acknowledge the reality of the death and remember the person who died.

- When possible, try not to use generic terms such as "your brother." Instead, use the name or nickname (with permission; sometimes nicknames are special) of the person who died.

CARPE DIEM

Look up the name of the person who died in a baby book and tell the child the meaning of the name. Ask her how this fits or doesn't fit with the person's personality.

38.

IMAGINE WHAT THE PERSON WHO DIED WOULD DO OR SAY

- If the grieving child is struggling with a decision or issue, ask him what the person who died would do or say.

- The child can imagine the person is still alive or the person is giving advice from heaven.

- Sometimes this leads to an anecdote or discussion of the person's life. Sometimes this gives the child a new perspective on the issue.

- Either way, it's mourning and it's healthy!

CARPE DIEM

Bring up a recent event in the child's life and ask him what the person who died would have done or said.

39.

LET THIS CHILD FEEL WHAT SHE FEELS. IF SHE SEEMS TO FEEL NUMB. . .

- As you might expect, children often initially feel a sense of shock or numbness when someone loved dies.

- This numbness is healthy because it protects the child from letting in too much of the pain and reality at once.

- Don't be offended even if the child seems *indifferent* to the death, especially at first. This is a normal and necessary survival tactic. With your help, she will confront her pain in doses as she feels ready.

CARPE DIEM

If other adults in the child's life are upset about her apparent lack of feelings about the death, talk to them about her normal need to confront the reality of the death as she feels ready.

40.

LET THIS CHILD FEEL WHAT HE FEELS. IF HE SEEMS TO BE ACTING BABYISH. . .

- When they're under the psychological stress of grief, children often want to return to the complete sense of security they felt earlier in life.

- It's normal for grieving kids to want to be held and rocked, sleep with parents, not leave their parents' side, ask to be fed or dressed, or pretend to be sick so they'll be taken care of.

- Don't make the grieving child feel ashamed of these behaviors. Instead, indulge them in the early days and weeks after the death.

- If the child is supported in his grief journey, regressive behaviors will normally disappear. If they don't, take this as a sign that something's amiss and that the child needs extra help.

CARPE DIEM

Hug and hold this child often. Today, give him a piggyback ride.

41.

LET THIS CHILD FEEL WHAT SHE FEELS. IF SHE SEEMS TO FEEL SCARED . . .

- Grieving kids often feel afraid.

- When the reality begins to set in that a significant person in the child's life will not be coming back, she may feel scared of not being taken care of or that someone else (or she!) will die, too.

- Assure the child that she will be loved and taken care of. And while you can't assure her that someone else she loves won't die, you can help her understand how long people normally live.

CARPE DIEM

Help the child make a plan for what to do when she feels afraid, such as saying a special prayer, hugging a favorite stuffed animal, or spending time with a grown-up she trusts.

42.

LET THIS CHILD FEEL WHAT HE FEELS. IF HE SEEMS TO FEEL ANGRY. . .

- The grieving child's explosive emotions—including not just anger but feelings of hate, blame, rage and jealousy—can be upsetting and threatening to adults because they are often uncertain how to respond.

- Often these feelings are simply a way for the child to protest the reality of the death. For example, the child may be angry (with God, with doctors) if someone he loved died an early death due to terminal illness.

- Don't make him feel such feelings are bad; instead, accept them and help him express them.

- Allowing the child to appropriately express his anger helps him survive during this difficult time. Find outlets for the child's explosive emotions. Talking can help, as can journaling, drawing and sports and other physical activities.

CARPE DIEM

Buy the child a small punching bag to hang in his room. Taking his anger out by boxing a punching bag is not only good therapy, it's good exercise!

43.

LET THIS CHILD FEEL WHAT SHE FEELS. IF SHE SEEMS TO BE ACTING TOO GROWN UP. . .

- Grieving kids act overly mature for a variety of reasons.

- Sometimes taking on a mother's role, for example, is the daughter's way of keep Mom alive. And it probably feels like something positive to do in the face of hopelessness and helplessness.

- Many times, however, it is adults who encourage (or force) grieving kids to act grown up. We do this when we don't have the energy to deal with appropriately childlike behavior or we inappropriately are looking for someone to fill in for the person who died.

- Try to discern the cause of the child's overmaturity, then express your concern both to her and her parents or guardians.

CARPE DIEM

Do something appropriately childlike with the grieving child today. Take her to the park or play tag with her.

44.

LET THIS CHILD FEEL WHAT SHE FEELS. IF SHE'S BEHAVING BADLY . . .

- Many children express the pain of grief through acting-out, which is simply the counselor's term for misbehavior.

- Rowdiness, temper tantrums, fighting with other kids, getting poor grades in school and defiance are typical acting-out behaviors in grieving kids.

- The grieving child often misbehaves because she feels insecure or abandoned or is trying to get a reaction out of adult caregivers who may otherwise be neglecting her.

- Try to understand the reasons behind this child's misbehavior, then supportively confront her about her inappropriate actions. As always, setting clear limits is a good idea.

CARPE DIEM

Make an agreement with the misbehaving child. When she feels like doing this, instead she'll do this…

45.

LET THIS CHILD FEEL WHAT HE FEELS. IF HE SEEMS TO FEEL LIKE HE'S TO BLAME...

- It is very human for both adults and children to blame themselves when someone they love dies.

- Young children are susceptible to magical thinking; they believe that by thinking about something they can make it happen. What child, for example, hasn't wished his sibling would go away forever? If the sibling dies, the child may feel he's to blame.

- The child may blame himself for any number of things, from not "saving" the person who died to still being alive even though the other person is dead.

- Help the child express his guilt, then reinforce that his thoughts didn't cause the person's death and he is in no way responsible for it.

CARPE DIEM

Ask the child why he thinks the person died. This question may reveal any guilty feelings he has.

46.

LET THIS CHILD FEEL WHAT SHE FEELS. IF SHE SEEMS TO FEEL RELIEVED. . .

- At times, grieving kids very appropriately experience a sense of relief when someone dies.

- Death can bring relief from suffering after an illness. The child's normal egocentrism may also cause her to feel relieved that now *she'll* finally get some attention. The child who has been physically, emotionally or sexually abused will also likely feel relief if the perpetrator dies.

- Whatever its source, relief is a natural and normal grief response. Help the child express her relief and let her know that her feelings are OK.

CARPE DIEM

If you or someone else also feels relief about the death, tell this to the child. This will help her understand that her feelings are normal.

47.

LET THIS CHILD FEEL WHAT HE FEELS. IF HE SEEMS TO FEEL VERY SAD. . .

- This dimension of grief is often the most difficult for grieving kids. Sadness, emptiness and depression often fully surface when the child really realizes the dead person will not be coming back.

- The child may feel the deepest sense of loss and emptiness long after adults in the child's life think grief support is necessary—typically months after the death.

- As hard as it is, grieving children need to embrace and express their sadness. They cannot be protected from it; if they are encouraged to avoid the pain, it will only surface later on and complicate their journey to adulthood.

CARPE DIEM

Observe the child today. Is he teaching you about his sadness through his play or other behaviors?

48.

LET THIS CHILD FEEL WHAT SHE FEELS. IF SHE SEEMS TO BE HAPPY . . .

- Children will be children, even after a death.

- Grieving kids still need to laugh and play each and every day. Play is their work, their way of learning and growing.

- Keep in mind that the grieving child's happiness does not mean she is "over" the death or "doing well" with her grief. She is probably just taking a much-needed break.

CARPE DIEM

Do something fun with the child today. Enjoy the moment.

49.

IF THE CHILD'S BODY HURTS, CONSIDER THIS

- At a time of acute grief, a child's body responds to what the mind has been told. Among the more common physical symptoms a grieving child exhibits are:

  - fatigue, lack of energy
  - difficulty sleeping or sometimes excessive sleeping
  - lack of appetite
  - shortness of breath
  - general nervousness, trembling
  - headaches
  - stomach pain

- Assure the grieving child that it's normal for his body to feel unwell right now. Take him in for a check-up if you think a doctor's OK will ease his fears.

CARPE DIEM

Schedule a well-child check-up today. Call the doctor in advance and explain to him the reason for the visit. Explain that you'd like the child's physical complaints to be taken seriously, but that if everything looks OK, the doctor should be as reassuring as possible.

50.

DON'T FALL BACK ON EUPHEMISMS

- Children can cope with what they know; they cannot cope with what they don't know.

- Don't lie to children or use euphemisms about death to try to protect them. Instead, use plain, honest words. Offer explanations at a level developmentally appropriate for them.

- For example, don't say, "Grandma has passed away"; say, "Grandma has died." Explain what dead means. You may also need to explain what will happen to the body, how and where it will be disposed of, etc.

- Avoid clichés such as "It was God's will" or "He wouldn't have wanted you to be sad" because they minimize the child's need to mourn.

CARPE DIEM

If the child seems curious, explain the cause of the death to her—even if the death was traumatic, violent or self-inflicted.

51.

DO SAY THIS

- I'm sorry.

- I'm thinking of you.

- I care.

- I love you.

- You are so important to me.

- I'm here for you.

- I want to help.

CARPE DIEM

Today, tell the child you love him. Do the same thing
tomorrow, and the next day, and the next . . .

52.

SPEND A SPECIAL DAY TOGETHER

- A few weeks after the death, maybe you can spend a special day with the grieving child—just the two of you.

- You don't need to go anywhere fabulous or do anything extraordinary. Instead, simply spend the day together doing things that allow you to talk and be close.

- Take the child out of school for the day if appropriate. It's good to let her know that grief and mourning—as well as her relationships with people who care about her—take precedence over school sometimes.

CARPE DIEM

Schedule and plan your day together. Make arrangements with the child's teacher or other caregivers if necessary.

53.

FIND A LOCAL SUPPORT GROUP FOR GRIEVING KIDS

- Support groups help grieving children by:

  - making them feel less alone in their grief.

  - providing emotional, physical and spiritual support in a safe, non-judgmental environment.

  - encouraging members to not only receive support for themselves, but also to provide help to others.

  - offering new ways of approaching problems.

  - helping them trust again.

  - rekindling their love for life and living.

- Check the child's school as well as your area hospice for support groups for grieving kids.

CARPE DIEM

Call around to find a support group for grieving kids, then talk to the group leader about the appropriateness of the group for this child.

54.

HAVE THE CHILD TALK
TO A COUNSELOR

- Some grieving kids may need or benefit from the extra layer of support provided by a counselor. The warning signs described in Idea 55 probably warrant a counselor's assessment, though "normal" grief can also be supported through counseling.

- Look for a counselor experienced in helping grieving kids. Some counselors are even certified in grief counseling.

- Consider family counseling if the entire family has been impacted by the death.

CARPE DIEM

Make inquiries about local counselors who might be appropriate for this child. That way you'll have the information handy if and when the need arises.

55.

WATCH FOR WARNING SIGNS

- For a variety of reasons, sometimes a child's grief gets complicated.

- If you see the following behaviors in a grieving child, it's probably a sign that he needs extra help with his thoughts and feelings:

    - total denial of the reality of the death

    - persistent panic, fear

    - chronic depression

    - chronic misbehavior

    - consistent withdrawal from friends and family

    - drug or alcohol abuse

    - suicidal thoughts or actions

- Listen to your gut. If it's telling you that this kid is in trouble, get help for him right away.

CARPE DIEM

If you notice any of these warning signs, alert the child's
network of adult caregivers as soon as possible. Ask
them to help you observe and support the child.

56.

HELP THE CHILD'S FAMILY MOURN

- The family's response to the death will play a crucial role in the child's mourning and healing.

- If the family is open and loving even in the face of death, the child will probably be taught how and encouraged to mourn.

- If the family doesn't talk about death and tends to repress feelings, the child will have a hard time mourning well on his own.

- If appropriate, talk to the child's parents or primary caregivers about their grief. Help the family and you'll be helping the child.

CARPE DIEM

Observe the mourning style of the child's family. Recommend family counseling if you think it would help.

57.

HELP THE CHILD AT SCHOOL

- Often grieving kids have a rough time at school. If the teacher is supportive, she may ease the child's re-entry into school after the death. But later on the child may feel ignored or even be teased.

- Make sure the child's teacher understands the circumstances of the death and the role the person who died played in the child's life.

- Give the teacher suggestions for helping this child at school. She may want to lead ongoing discussions about death or have the kids write essays about their own grief experiences, for example.

- The grieving child's performance at school may naturally suffer. It's normal—even desirable—for the child to focus on grief and mourning for a time before he can start concentrating on school again.

CARPE DIEM

Call the child's teacher for an update on the child's school life. Call her at regular intervals in the coming months.

58.

EASE THE CHILD'S RELATIONSHIPS WITH HER PEERS

- Kids can be tough on other kids, especially when they sense a weak spot or difference. Grief can create such a difference.

- Talk to the grieving child about her friendships. Ask her if her friends are being supportive or if they're acting weird. Give her some words for talking to them about the death.

- Have the child's teacher talk to her friends about the death and how they can help.

- Invite some friends over to the grieving child's house and help make it a fun time.

CARPE DIEM

Help throw a party for the child and her friends.

59.

BE THE CHILD'S ADVOCATE

- Think of yourself as the grieving child's advocate. Even if you aren't around him all the time, you can still take steps to ensure that his other environments are supportive and friendly.

- Sometimes a few simple phone calls is all it takes to alert other adults in the child's life to his special needs right now.

- Consider the following spheres of influence: immediate family, extended family, neighborhood, school, circle of friends, extracurricular activities and church.

CARPE DIEM

Write thank you notes to all the adults who are helping this child right now. If you affirm their support, it will likely continue.

60.

HELP THE CHILD MAKE
A MEMORY BOOK

- A memory book is a photo album or scrapbook filled with memories of the person who died.

- Help the child compile a memory book that's just for her. Buy the materials then set aside an hour or two to put it together.

- For her memory book, the child could select photos, drawings, souvenirs and anything else that helps her remember the person who died.

CARPE DIEM

Today, visit your local craft or stationery store and buy the materials you'll need for the memory book. Don't forget glue, photo corners, photo sleeves and fine-point markers for captions.

61.

HELP THE CHILD PACK
A MEMORY BOX

- A memory box is even easier than a memory book; you simply put things that remind the child of the person who died in a special box. The box can be as big or as small as you want.

- Maybe you can help the child decorate a box if he likes art projects. He could draw pictures of memories on the outside of the box or wrap it in scraps of fabric from clothing that the person who died wore.

- Help the child fill the box with pictures, souvenirs, videotapes and things that belonged to the person who died.

CARPE DIEM

Find a good box to use as a memory box. Look for something sturdy that will stand up to years of a child's loving touch.

62.

ENCOURAGE THE CHILD TO WRITE DOWN HER FEELINGS

- Even by age six, many children can read and write well enough to begin to keep a journal. Grief journals help kids express their thoughts and feelings; writing them down is a form of mourning.

- If the thought of a whole journal is overwhelming for this child, how about suggesting that she write a story or a poem?

- Sometimes grieving kids like to write a letter to the person who died. In the letter they can share the thoughts and feelings they've had since the death. They can also "update" the person who died on their life since the death. Ask the child to read the letter aloud to you or to another trusted adult.

CARPE DIEM

Give the child an empty notebook to use as her journal. Your local bookstore or stationery store probably has blank books with pretty covers.

63.

SEND THE CHILD A CARD OR LETTER

- Kids love to get mail, and grieving kids are no exception.

- A quick note or postcard lets the child know you are thinking about him and you care about him. But don't send just one! Send a half dozen in the coming months.

- To mark special occasions, you might want to include a gift certificate to the child's favorite store at the mall or tickets for two (you and him!) to a play or sporting event.

- Don't forget e-mail! Lots of kids are online today.

CARPE DIEM

Buy 5 or 6 cards all at once and drop the first one in the mail to the child today. Save the others for the coming months.

64.

SEND THE CHILD A CARE PACKAGE

- Children love to get mail but they really love to get packages.

- Even if the grieving child lives nearby and especially if she doesn't, send her a care package.

- Include her favorite treats, maybe an article of clothing, a CD, a toothbrush—stuff she'll use and other stuff just for fun.

- Don't forget a supportive note from you!

CARPE DIEM

Stop by your local variety store today and pick up some items for the child's care package. Or make a batch of her favorite cookies!

65.

FRAME THE PERSON WHO DIED

- It's good for the grieving child to look at pictures of the person who died and to have them displayed around his room or house.

- Help the child preserve those precious snapshots by buying a few special frames.

- Also consider enlarging a few special photos to 9x10 or even poster size for the child's room. Again, buy frames (perhaps with archival quality matting and glass) so the photos will last throughout the child's life. Twenty years from now they'll be irreplaceable keepsakes.

CARPE DIEM

Buy the child a small photo album then help him insert photos of the person who died. He may want to keep the album near his bed or in his memory box.

66.

BE ARTISTS TOGETHER

- Sometimes grief unleashes the budding artist in all of us.

- If the grieving child likes to do artwork, take her interest seriously. Buy her some good quality equipment for her favorite medium.

- Encourage her to follow through by creating art together. You paint on your canvas while she paints on hers.

- The child's artwork doesn't always have to be directly about her grief, but her moods and feelings will naturally come through in her art.

CARPE DIEM

Sign up for a community education art class together. One that meets over several weeks will give her something to look forward to.

67.

PLANT A GARDEN TOGETHER

- Most kids love to plant flowers and vegetables and watch them grow.

- Planting and tending a garden gets the grieving child outside and gives her an activity to look forward to all summer long.

- In the spring, help the child plan and plant a small garden. Or, if you're not the gardener in the child's life, suggest this activity to the person who is!

- To the Victorians, certain flowers signified certain emotions. Maybe you can help the child choose plants that reflect her journey through grief.

CARPE DIEM

Give the child a houseplant for her room. Ask your florist to help you choose one that will need little upkeep. Cactuses and succulents are good bets because they'll survive on almost no water!

68.

LISTEN TO MUSIC TOGETHER

- Sometimes grieving kids like to listen to music alone (witness the pre-teen, headphones on head, jamming to his iPod), but sometimes they like for you to hear "their" music.

- Pay attention to music the grieving child is listening to. Read the lyrics. Is it appropriate for this child at this time?

- Expose the child to different kinds of music. Take him to hear the orchestra or a jazz pianist.

- Consider listening together to favorite music of the person who died.

CARPE DIEM

Buy the child the CD he's been coveting.

69.

PLAY A QUIET GAME TOGETHER

- In this era of raucous video games and televised football, we sometimes forget how much fun a simple board or card game can be.

- Teach the child how to play cribbage or Monopoly or chess—or checkers for the younger ones!

- Quiet moments together are good opportunities for the child to update you on her thoughts and feelings.

CARPE DIEM

Go through your closets and select a game you think the child might like to play. Ask her to join you this afternoon.

70.

PLAY AN ACTIVE GAME TOGETHER

- Kids love it when grown-ups summon up the energy to get active with them. It's a great way to build trust!

- Do something active together that this child enjoys. You can simply play tag or catch in the backyard. Orchestrate a game of Simon Says or Kick the Can with a few other kids. Or go on a bike ride, play tennis or frisbee golf, or take a long hike somewhere picturesque.

- Active games can be a good way for grieving kids to express explosive emotions.

CARPE DIEM

Introduce the child to a game he's never played
before, such as croquet or horseshoes.

71.

PLAY OUTSIDE TOGETHER

- There's something about the openness, the light and the air that makes outside the best place to play.

- In the summer you can swim, throw water balloons, blow bubbles, pick dandelions and skip rocks across the pond.

- In the winter you can sled, make snowmen, have a snowball fight and go ice skating.

CARPE DIEM

Do something seasonal outside today with the child.

72.

EXPLORE NATURE TOGETHER

- I find spending time in nature very healing. When I take grieving kids for mountain hikes around my Center, they seem to respond.

- Would this child like to go camping with you? Pack a tent, sleeping bags and other essentials and rough it for a night or two.

- Other ideas: visit the zoo; collect insects; row a boat on a nearby lake.

- Take advantage of the solitude. Now is a good time to talk to the child about her thoughts and feelings.

CARPE DIEM

Pick up a local hiking trails map and take the
child on a one- or two-mile hike.

73.

SURF THE WEB TOGETHER

- There's a whole world of grief information and support at your fingertips; just get plugged in to the Web!

- Children need supervision when surfing the Web, especially when they're emotionally vulnerable.

- Check out these Web sites: www.griefnet.org and www.kidsaid.com. The former is more appropriate for adult helpers; the latter is for grieving kids.

CARPE DIEM

Type "kids AND grief" into your favorite
search engine. See what comes up.

74.

COOK SOMETHING TOGETHER

- Kids usually don't like to cook when it's presented as a chore, but when they're enthusiastically invited to help prepare a special treat, they'll eagerly don an apron.

- Cook a meal for someone who would appreciate it, perhaps a busy mom or a lonely neighbor. Pack it in a box complete with condiments, festive napkins and a centerpiece.

- Pass along a favorite family recipe to the child. Help him prepare it then sit down and enjoy it together!

- Consider making favorite foods of the person who died—maybe in honor of the person's birthday.

CARPE DIEM

What's the child's favorite dessert? Buy the ingredients and help him prepare it tonight.

75.

DO A PROJECT TOGETHER

- What makes this child's clock tick? Think about her interests then invite her to do a project with you.

- Pick something you can complete in an afternoon (maybe a memory book; see Idea 60) or, even better, something the two of you can work on together in the coming weeks and months.

- Some ideas: build a bookcase for the childs' room; plant a terrarium; make holiday gifts for her friends; put together a 2,000 piece puzzle; research her family tree.

CARPE DIEM

Plan a project the two of you can work on next time you're together.

76.

ENTER A CONTEST TOGETHER

- It's important for mourners—adults and kids alike—to have ongoing goals and things to look forward to. Otherwise, why get your feet out of bed in the morning?

- Contests help us set our sights ahead. There's nothing like a prize to get people motivated!

- Keep your eyes open for contests that might appeal to this child. Maybe you could help him write an essay or enter a soapbox derby. Or train to enter a running or biking race together.

CARPE DIEM

Carefully scan the newspaper for upcoming local contests or races.
Talk to the child about his interest in participating with you.

77.

DO SOMETHING "OLD-FASHIONED" TOGETHER

- Kids can be fascinated by "the way things were." And learning about the past gives them a new perspective on the present and the future.

- What did you love to do when you were a kid? Introduce the child to a vintage toy or activity from your childhood.

- Bake a cake from scratch. Go caroling during the holidays or make a May basket for your neighbors. Visit an old one-room schoolhouse or a local museum.

CARPE DIEM

Pretend it's the 1800s. No TV, no video games, no electricity. Light candles at nightfall and read *Little Women* or *Robinson Crusoe* aloud.

78.

START AND BUILD A COLLECTION TOGETHER

- Collecting things is a human need; it gives us a feeling of control and expertise—healthy feelings the grieving child is probably low on right now.

- As always, start with what interests the child. Does she like dolls? Outdoorsy things? Sports? Books?

- Help her learn about her collection and earn money to buy new items. Maybe the two of you could even build a display case for her room.

- Collections don't have to cost money. Kids can collect rocks, feathers, leaves or flowers (for pressing), insects, etc.

CARPE DIEM

Take the child out today and start off her collection.

79.

PLAY DRESS-UP TOGETHER

- Halloween and the occasional grown-ups' costume party remind us that dressing up can be a blast for any age and either gender.

- Younger kids are often enthusiastic about dressing up as dancers, pirates, knights, damsels and many other fantasy characters. Let them pick a costume for you then take part in the imaginative game that follows!

- Older kids' taste for dress-up gets more sophisticated. Take them clothes shopping at your local thrift store and see what happens. Retro is very cool, you know.

CARPE DIEM

Buy two sets of Groucho Marx nose and glasses. Teach the child who Marx was and show him his mannerisms.

80.

DECORATE THE CHILD'S ROOM TOGETHER

- Kids feel empowered when their bedrooms are their rooms—a safe, personalized place for sleeping, playing, thinking and dreaming.

- Help the child decorate his room. Ask him what colors he likes, what he'd like to have hanging on the walls. Take him shopping with you for paint, wallpaper and posters. Let him choose!

- Refrain from being an arbiter of good taste. If he really wants electric blue walls, that's OK. Remember—it's only paint. (Or offer to paint one wall a dramatic color and the others more subdued tones.) The point is to let him take ownership of his space and, by extension, his life.

CARPE DIEM

Tear out some pictures of kids' rooms from decorating magazines. Show them to the child and see if he connects with any of them.

81.

STAY UP LATE TOGETHER

- Do you remember when you first stayed up until midnight? 3 a.m.? All night long? (And bragged about it to your friends the next day?) Such fatiguing feats are rites of passage for children.

- Spend an evening with the child and let her stay up as late as she wants to. Play cards or watch an old movie together. Make popcorn—on the stove! Order pizza in the wee hours of the morning.

- Spread out sleeping bags on the living room floor and have a camp-in. First one to sleep is a rotten egg!

CARPE DIEM

If tonight's not a school night, invite the child to stay up late with you. Put together a survival kit of munchies, movies, music and games.

82.

LAUGH TOGETHER

- Oh, please do! I hope that you're willing to laugh and have fun as much as this child wants to!

- When he's in the mood, get giggly with him. Make faces and tell jokes. Play harmless pranks on others.

- Laughter gives us hope. The grieving child who understands that love and laughter are still possible in his life is the grieving child who can look forward to his future.

CARPE DIEM

Memorize an age-appropriate joke and tell it to the child today.

83.

TEACH THE CHILD
SOMETHING NEW

- Is there something this child has always wanted to learn how to do? Ask her.

- If she's interested, teach her something you're good at. When she loses interest it's time to move on.

- Maybe both of you can learn to do something that the person who died liked to do.

CARPE DIEM

Ask the child to make a list of 10 things she'd like to learn how to do. Together pick one thing and make it a reality!

84.

TAKE THE CHILD SOMEPLACE NEW

- New places teach us new things and give us new perspectives on our old, familiar haunts.

- Take the child someplace he's never been before. Drive to a nearby town or, when possible and appropriate, fly to a new part of the country (or the world!) for a few days' respite.

- You don't need to leave town to go someplace new. Take the child to a local restaurant, store, museum or park where he's never been before.

- Some grieving kids will be more willing to open up to you when they're "unstuck" from their usual places and routines.

CARPE DIEM

Tell the child you're taking him somewhere special, blindfold him then drive him somewhere he's never been before. Make it no more than a 15 minute trip. Along the way, give him clues.

85.

VOLUNTEER WITH THE CHILD

- Volunteerism is a way of promoting self-worth and a sense of purpose.

- Most communities have lots of volunteer opportunities for kids, especially when adults are willing to help.

- Call your area United Way and ask if there's a local nonprofit or upcoming event in need of two extra pairs of hands. Explain that you and a child want to work together. Other places to try: your church or the child's school.

CARPE DIEM

Check the local newspaper for calls for volunteers.

86.

CONSPIRE TO HELP SOMEONE ELSE

- What's more fun than sharing a secret?

- Ask the grieving child if there's someone she'd like to do something nice for. Help her plan and carry out a top-secret, random act of kindness. If the child enjoys playing benefactress, conspire to help another person, then another…

- Maybe the two of you could "adopt" someone who needs long-term support. Do you have an elderly neighbor who needs help around the house? Does the child know a new student at school who just moved to town?

CARPE DIEM

Talk to the child about whom she'd like to
help. Begin making plans today.

87.

LET THE CHILD ALONE

- A caution: If you were to follow all the guidelines in this book and to complete each and every recommended activity with the grieving child, you would smother her!

- Grieving kids do need the love, support and ongoing presence of caring adults. But they also need down time. They need to hang out with other kids and they need time to be alone.

- When the child teaches you she wants you to leave her alone (perhaps by retreating to her room or by defying you), respect her need for distance.

- Intermittent and short-lived bouts of rebellion are normal. Grieving kids who withdraw for days and weeks at a time, however, need intervention and extra help.

CARPE DIEM

The next time the child rebels, keep your distance. She'll let you know when she's ready for your company again.

88.

LOVE THE OTHER
CHILDREN/PEOPLE IN YOUR LIFE

- Helping a grieving child is indeed an honorable and rewarding goal. I thank you, society thanks you and, in time, the child will thank you.

- But don't focus so much on helping this grieving child that you neglect the other important people in your life.

- Your family, your friends and your coworkers all need your support and presence, too.

- Last but not least, don't forget to love yourself and to make time for you.

CARPE DIEM

Who have you been neglecting lately? Spend
some quality time with this person today.

89.

TELL THE CHILD A STORY

- Kids are enchanted when grown-ups enter their world of imagination and play.

- Tell the grieving child a story. Make it up as you go along.

- Ask the child to choose the main characters. They can be people, animals, pretend creatures, even inanimate objects (which you'll make come alive in your story!).

- If you can pull it off, weave a story with facts and characters from the child's own life. Make sure it has a happy ending!

CARPE DIEM

Instead of reading to the child before bed tonight,
make up a story. Turn off the lights and snuggle
with her while exercising your imagination!

90.

BE COMPASSIONATE

- You probably wouldn't be helping a grieving child if you weren't compassionate, but even we caregiver types can use a refresher course in compassion now and then!

- Compassion grows from empathy, which involves projecting ourselves into the child's world and viewing the situation through the child's eyes.

- To have empathy also is to understand the meaning of the child's experience instead of imposing meaning on that experience from the outside.

- Acting on your empathy is being compassionate.

CARPE DIEM

Compassionate literally means "with passion." Care
for this child "with passion" today.

91.

BE GENUINE

- You can't really help the grieving child unless you can be genuine with him. Kids can smell a phony a mile away.

- Be yourself. Be honest.

- You don't have to be good at everything (or the kind of person who could pull off all the suggestions in this book) to help the grieving child; you just need to help in ways that feel comfortable for you.

CARPE DIEM

What are you good at? What are you not so good at? An honest assessment of your strengths and weaknesses will help you decide how best you can help this child.

92.

BE SPONTANEOUS

- As much as kids need structure and routine, they also crave spontaneity. In fact, children are spontaneity incarnate! (Have you ever observed kids bouncing from one place and one activity to another when they have a free day?)

- Be spontaneous with the grieving child. Take her somewhere unplanned and unannounced. Wake her up early one Saturday morning and take her on a surprise excursion.

- Instead of imposing order on the child's life all the time, every once in a while be the czar of disorder. Decree today a day of mismatched clothes. Roll around in the grass instead of mowing it. Skip dinner and go straight to dessert.

CARPE DIEM

Surprise the child with a special gift or activity today.

93.

BE SILLY

- Grief and mourning are so darned serious. Sometimes grieving kids need to set down the weight of grief and get crazy.

- Invite the child to be silly. Show him you can be just as nutty as he can!

- Make faces. Act like a monkey. Use physical humor.

CARPE DIEM

Rent a silly movie and watch it with the grieving child. Kids often appreciate the slapstick antics of The Three Stooges!

94.

BE THERE ON SPECIAL DAYS AND OCCASIONS

- Certain days are bound to be hard for the grieving child, such as the child's birthday, the birthday of the person who died, the anniversary of the death, holidays, and once-in-a-lifetime events such as school plays and graduations.

- These days remind the child that an important person in his life can't be there for him.

- Acknowledge the loss on these days by telling the child, "Your mother would be so proud of you" or "Your brother (use the name) loved Christmas cookies, didn't he?"

CARPE DIEM

Right now, while you're thinking about it, mark these special days on your planning calendar. Make a note to support the child somehow on those days.

95.

PLAN A CEREMONY
WITH THE CHILD

- Funeral ceremonies are powerful rituals for adults and children alike (see Idea 9). But ceremonies held long after the death can also be healing.

- The anniversary of the death might be a good time for mourners to get together. Hold hands around a table with a large candle lit in the center. One by one share a memory of the person who died. As each person speaks he lights a small votive candle by holding it to the center candle's flame. This ceremony is appropriate for all ages (of course, younger children will need help with their candles).

- Often children like to do something in honor of the person who died. Offer to organize a tree planting ceremony. Together with other mourners, plant a tree somewhere meaningful to the person who died. The child can help dig the hole and water in the sapling. An engraved marker in the ground near the tree makes a lasting tribute.

CARPE DIEM

When you talk to the child, broach the subject of planning a ceremony. If she seems interested, begin planning one with her.

96.

BE PREPARED FOR "GRIEFBURSTS"

- Sometimes sudden, unexpected and strong waves of sadness will overtake the child. These "griefbursts" can happen even long after the event of the death.

- Griefbursts are normal but can be very scary and disheartening for the child. "But I was having fun and feeling so much better!" he might think to himself.

- Encourage him to talk to a grown-up when a griefburst bursts in. Maybe you can sit with him quietly until it passes.

CARPE DIEM

Make a game plan for what you'll do if and when
the child experiences a griefburst.

97.

DON'T SET A TIMETABLE FOR THE CHILD'S GRIEF

- Just as there is no one "right way" to mourn, there is no correct timetable for the journey through grief.

- Some children will experience intense grief for months and months, especially if the person who died was a parent or sibling or best friend.

- Active mourning helps grief proceed.

- In general, as time passes and as the child is loved and helped to mourn, the intensity and duration of the child's feelings of grief will soften. This is a sign that reconciliation is unfolding.

CARPE DIEM

Help other important adults in the child's life understand
that the grief journey may take a long, long time.

98.

UNDERSTAND THAT CHILDREN DON'T "GET OVER" GRIEF

- As humans, we don't ever "get over" grief. It changes us irrevocably. We are never the same after the death of someone loved.

- But we can and do learn to "reconcile" our grief. That is, we learn to live with it and to incorporate what we have learned from it into our continued living.

- Grieving kids don't "get over" grief, either. As they learn and grow, they adapt to it anew.

- Each milestone in the child's life (first award, travel to new places, move to a new home, graduation, marriage, etc.) may be bittersweet as he revisits his grief and reinterprets how the loss has affected his life.

CARPE DIEM

Think about deaths you experienced earlier in life. Have you "gotten over" them? How do the people who died continue to be a presence in your life?

99.

SUPPORT AND LOVE THIS CHILD FOR YEARS TO COME

- Grief never ends. You can help by being a loving, supportive, reliable presence in the child's life in the coming months and years.

- As the grieving child begins to heal, she will need your focused help less often. But if you are an important part of her young life, she will want to share her ongoing challenges and triumphs with you!

- Don't drop out of the child's life, even when she seems to be busy with other things. Ongoing notes and birthday cards are sure to be appreciated.

CARPE DIEM

Even long after the death, call the child out of the blue and ask her how she's doing. Tell her you're thinking about her and that you love her.

100.

BELIEVE IN THE CHILD'S CAPACITY TO HEAL

- The most important quality you bring to the table in your work with grieving kids is your belief in the child's capacity to heal.

- If you truly believe that this child can heal and go on to live a happy, full life, your optimism will color every moment you spend with the child.

- Children are resilient, strong, amazing creatures. With lots of love and support, they can not only heal in grief, they can grow as a result of it.

CARPE DIEM

Be a witness to this child's healing. As you see her making strides forward, congratulate her and honor her progress.

A FINAL WORD

There is good reason to have hope that grieving children can integrate death into their lives and go on to live well and love well again. With ample love and support, they can and they do. Many times I have been privileged to see children not only heal but grow through grief. They often emerge emotionally and spiritually stronger, more adaptable, more appreciative of life's joys. They become beautiful, healthy, life-loving adults.

I sometimes liken grieving kids to flowers. Then in the last sentence of that graph, delete the words like the daisy. Like a flower after a hard spring rain, grieving children often feel fragile and battered at first. To grow, the flower needs sun and the gentle tending of the gardener. The kids need love and the help of adults like you. When they get what they need, they open wide and soak up the sunshine of life.

I hope we meet one day and that you will share your experiences helping grieving kids with me. Until then, best wishes and Godspeed.

THE GRIEVING CHILD'S
BILL OF RIGHTS

(Please share this with a grieving child you care about.)

1. **I have the right to have my own unique feelings about the death.** I might feel mad, sad or lonely. I might feel scared or relieved. I might feel numb or sometimes not anything at all. No one will feel exactly like I do.

2. **I have the right to talk about my grief whenever I feel like talking.** When I need to talk, I will find someone who will listen to me and love me. When I don't want to talk, that's OK, too.

3. **I have the right to show my feelings of grief in my own way.** When they are hurting, some kids like to play so they'll feel better for awhile. I can play or laugh, too. I might also get mad and misbehave. This does not mean I am bad, it just means I have scary feelings that I need help with.

4. **I have the right to need other people to help me with my grief, especially grown-ups who care about me.** Mostly I need them to pay attention to what I am feeling and saying and to love me no matter what.

5. **I have the right to get upset about normal, everyday problems.** I might feel grumpy and have trouble getting along with others sometimes.

6. **I have the right to have "griefbursts."** Griefbursts are sudden, unexpected feelings of sadness that just hit me sometimes—even long after the death. These feelings can be very strong and even scary. When this happens, I might feel afraid to be alone.

7. **I have the right to use my beliefs about God to help me with my grief.** Praying might make me feel better and somehow closer to the person who died.

8. **I have the right to try to figure out *why* the person I loved died.** But it's OK if I don't find an answer. "Why" questions about life and death are the hardest questions in the world.

9. **I have the right to think and talk about my memories of the person who died.** Sometimes those memories will be happy and sometimes they might be sad. Either way, memories help me keep alive my love for the person who died.

10. **I have the right to move toward and feel my grief and, over time, to heal.** I'll go on to live a happy life, but the life and death of the person who died will always be a part of me. I'll always miss the person who died.

SEND US YOUR IDEAS
FOR HEALING A CHILD'S
GRIEVING HEART!

I'd love to hear your practical ideas for helping grieving kids. I may use them in other books some day. Please jot down your ideas and mail them to:

Dr. Alan Wolfelt
The Center for Loss and Life Transition
3735 Broken Bow Road
Fort Collins, CO 80526
DrWolfelt@centerforloss.com

I look forward to hearing from you!

My idea:

_____

_____

_____

_____

My name and mailing/e-mail address:

_____

_____

_____

ALSO BY ALAN WOLFELT

A Child's View of Grief

In this informative, easy-to-read booklet, Dr. Wolfelt explains how children and adolescents grieve after someone loved dies and offers helping guidelines for caregiving adults. An excellent, concise resource for parents of grieving kids.

ISBN 978-1-879651-43-2 • 45 pages • softcover • $6.95

Companion
PRESS

All Dr. Wolfelt's publications can be ordered by mail from:
Companion Press
3735 Broken Bow Road
Fort Collins, CO 80526
(970) 226-6050
www.centerforloss.com

ALSO BY ALAN WOLFELT

Healing Your Grieving Heart for Kids

100 Practical Ideas

Healing Your Grieving Heart for Kids is for young and middle readers (6-12 year-olds) grieving the death of someone loved. The text is simple and straightforward, teaching children about grief and affirming that their thoughts and feelings are not only normal but necessary. Page after page of age-appropriate activities and gentle, healing guidance.

ISBN 978-1-879651-27-2 • 128 pages • softcover • $11.95

Companion
PRESS

All Dr. Wolfelt's publications can be ordered by mail from:
Companion Press
3735 Broken Bow Road
Fort Collins, CO 80526
(970) 226-6050
www.centerforloss.com

ALSO BY ALAN WOLFELT

How I Feel

A Coloring Book for Grieving Children

Dr. Wolfelt's coloring book for kids ages 3-8 explores many of the feelings grieving children often experience. The expressive, easy-to-color drawings clearly depict disbelief, fear, anger, loneliness, happiness, sadness, and other normal grief feelings. And the simple text accompanying the drawings ("Someone I love has died;" "Ever since this person died, I have felt new and scary feelings. Grown-ups call these feelings grief;" "Sometimes I feel all alone;" "Sometimes I hurt inside") provides grieving children with words to describe their new, sometimes scary feelings.

ISBN 978-1-879651-17-3 • 22 pages • $2.00
(plus $2 shipping and handling for a single copy)

Bulk Order Discount • 25 copies • $30.00 (plus regular S&H)

Companion
P R E S S

All Dr. Wolfelt's publications can be ordered by mail from:
Companion Press
3735 Broken Bow Road
Fort Collins, CO 80526
(970) 226-6050
www.centerforloss.com

ALSO BY ALAN WOLFELT

Healing the Bereaved Child

Grief Gardening, Growth Through Grief and Other Touchstones for Caregivers

One spring morning a gardener noticed an unfamiliar seedling poking through the ground near the rocky, untended edge of his garden . . .

So begins the parable that sets the tone for this inspiring, heartfelt classic for caregivers to bereaved children. By comparing grief counseling to gardening, Dr. Wolfelt frees caregivers of the traditional medical model of bereavement care, which implies that grief is an illness that must be cured. He suggests that caregivers instead embrace a more holistic view of the normal, natural and necessary process that is grief. He then explores the ways in which bereaved children can not only heal but grow through grief.

Part textbook, part workbook, part meditation, this exhilarating guide is a must-read for child counselors, hospice caregivers, funeral directors, school counselors and teachers, clergy, parents—anyone who wants to offer support and companionship to children affected by the death of someone loved.

ISBN 978-1-879651-10-4
8 1/2" x 11" • 344 pages • softcover • $39.95

Companion
P R E S S

All Dr. Wolfelt's publications can be ordered by mail from:
Companion Press
3735 Broken Bow Road
Fort Collins, CO 80526
(970) 226-6050
www.centerforloss.com

ALSO BY ALAN WOLFELT

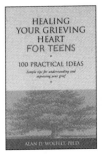

Healing Your Grieving Heart for Teens

100 Practical Ideas

In this compassionate book for grieving teenagers, Dr. Wolfelt speaks honestly and straightforwardly to teens, affirming their thoughts and feelings and giving them dozens of teen-friendly ideas for understanding and coping with their grief. The book also acknowledges teenagers' natural tendencies to spurn adult help while encouraging them to express their grief. Unlike longer, more text-dense books on grief, the one-idea-per-page format is inviting and readable for this age group.

ISBN 978-1-879651-23-4 • 128 pages • softcover • $11.95

Companion
PRESS

All Dr. Wolfelt's publications can be ordered by mail from:
Companion Press
3735 Broken Bow Road
Fort Collins, CO 80526
(970) 226-6050
www.centerforloss.com

ALSO BY ALAN WOLFELT

The Healing Your Grieving Heart Journal for Teens

With a Foreword by Brian Griese

Teenagers often don't want to talk to adults—or even to their friends—about their struggles. But given the opportunity, many will choose the more private option of writing. Many grieving teens find that journaling helps them sort through their confusing thoughts and feelings.

Yet few journals created just for teens exist and even fewer address the unique needs of the grieving teen. In the Introduction, this unique journal—written by Dr. Wolfelt and his 14-year-old daughter, Megan—affirms the grieving teen's thoughts and feelings and offers gentle, healing guidance. The six central needs of mourning are explained, as are common grief responses. Throughout, the authors provide simple, open-ended questions for the grieving teen to explore, such as:

- What do you miss most about the person who died?
- Write down one special memory.
- Which feelings have been most difficult for you since the death? Why?
- Is there something you wish you had said to the person who died but never did?
- Describe the personality of the person who died.

Designed just for grieving teens as a companion to Dr. Wolfelt's bestselling *Healing Your Grieving Heart for Teens: 100 Practical Ideas*, this journal will be a comforting, affirming and healing presence for teens in the weeks, months and years after the death of someone loved.

ISBN 978-1-879651-33-3 • 128 pages • softcover • $11.95

Companion
PRESS

All Dr. Wolfelt's publications can be ordered by mail from:
Companion Press
3735 Broken Bow Road
Fort Collins, CO 80526
(970) 226-6050
www.centerforloss.com

ALSO BY ALAN WOLFELT

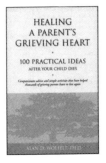

Healing A Parent's Grieving Heart

100 Practical Ideas After Your Child Dies

The unthinkable has happened: your child has died. How do you go on? What can you do with your pain? Where do you turn?

With a foreword by bereaved parent and editor of *Grief Digest* Andrea Gambill, this book offers 100 practical ideas that have helped other grieving parents understand and reconcile their grief. Common challenges, such as dealing with marital stress, helping surviving siblings, dealing with hurtful advice from others and exploring feelings of guilt, are also addressed.

ISBN 978-1-879651-30-2 • 128 pages • softcover • $11.95

Companion
PRESS

All Dr. Wolfelt's publications can be ordered by mail from:
Companion Press
3735 Broken Bow Road
Fort Collins, CO 80526
(970) 226-6050
www.centerforloss.com

ALSO BY ALAN WOLFELT

Living in the Shadow of the Ghosts of Grief
Step into the Light
Reconcile old losses and open the door to infinite joy and love

"Accumulated, unreconciled loss affects every aspect of our lives. Living in the Shadow is a beautifully written compass with the needle ever-pointing in the direction of hope."
— Greg Yoder, grief counselor

"So often we try to dance around our grief. This book offers the reader a safe place to do the healing work of "catch-up" mourning, opening the door to a life of freedom, authenticity and purpose."
— Kim Farris-Luke, bereavement coordinator

Are you depressed? Anxious? Angry? Do you have trouble with trust and intimacy? Do you feel a lack of meaning and purpose in your life? You may well be living in the shadow of the ghosts of grief.

When you suffer a loss of any kind—whether through abuse, divorce, job loss, the death of someone loved or other transitions, you naturally grieve inside. To heal your grief, you must express it. That is, you must mourn your grief. If you don't, you will carry your grief into your future, and it will undermine your happiness for the rest of your life.

This compassionate guide will help you learn to identify and mourn your carried grief so you can go on to live the joyful, whole life you deserve.

ISBN 978-1-879651-51-7 • 160 pages • softcover • $13.95

Companion
PRESS

All Dr. Wolfelt's publications can be ordered by mail from:
Companion Press
3735 Broken Bow Road
Fort Collins, CO 80526
(970) 226-6050
www.centerforloss.com

ALSO BY ALAN WOLFELT

The Journey Through Grief

Reflections On Healing
Second Edition

This popular hardcover book makes a wonderful gift for those who grieve, helping them gently engage in the work of mourning. Comforting and nurturing, *The Journey Through Grief* doses mourners with the six needs of mourning, helping them soothe themselves at the same time it helps them heal.

Back by popular demand, we are now offering *The Journey Through Grief* again in hardcover. The hardcover version of this beautiful book makes a wonderful, healing gift for the newly bereaved.

This revised, second edition of *The Journey Through Grief* takes Dr. Wolfelt's popular book of reflections and adds space for guided journaling, asking readers thoughtful questions about their unique mourning needs and providing room to write responses.

The Journey Through Grief is organized around the six needs that all mourners must yield to—indeed embrace—if they are to go on to find continued meaning in life and living. Following a short explanation of each mourning need is a series of brief, spiritual passages that, when read slowly and reflectively, help mourners work through their unique thoughts and feelings. *The Journey Through Grief* is being used by many faith communities as part of their grief support programs.

ISBN 978-1-879651-11-1 • hardcover • 176 pages • $21.95

Companion
P R E S S

All Dr. Wolfelt's publications can be ordered by mail from:
Companion Press
3735 Broken Bow Road
Fort Collins, CO 80526
(970) 226-6050
www.centerforloss.com